Stella Europa

by
Ian Grant

Cornwall Editions

First published 2015
by Cornwall Editions Ltd
52 Gladsmuir Road,
London N19 3JU

ISBN 978-1-904880-33-2

Stella Europa © Creative Structure Ltd 2015

Ian Grant has asserted his right under the Copyright, Designs and Patents Act, 1988, to be identified as the author of this work.

All rights reserved. No part of this publication may be reproduced or transmitted in any form or by any means, electronic or mechanical, including photocopying, recording, or any information storage or retrieval system, without prior written permission from the publisher.

Stella Europa is a work of fiction. Names, characters, places, organisations and events are either products of the author's imagination or used fictitiously.
This version of the text went to print before the end of rehearsals and may differ slightly from the version performed.

All professional enquiries regarding this play should be addressed to:

Creative Structure Ltd,
52 Gladsmuir Road,
Upper Holloway,
London N19 3JU, UK

www.creativestructure.net
ian.grant@creativestructure.net

+44 776 418 7452

Printed and bound by Lightning Source UK

The first performance of *Stella Europa* was given on 21 April 2015 at the Hen and Chickens Theatre, London.

The cast, in alphabetical order, was as follows

Jack Cameron	Lambros Fountoulis / Ally Erskine / Ted Barnes
Euan Forsyth	Robertson / Jimmy Kerridge
Steven Maddocks	Henry Anscombe
Isabelle Clara Mason	Kristina Winberg / Laura Anscombe / Angela Clissold
Laura Reeves	Beatrice Tremain / Tatiana / Amelia
Justin Stahley	Geert Wilders / John Dove / Jack Adams
Denise Stephenson	Marine Le Pen / Lady Mary Herbert / Celia Winstanley
Chris David Storer	Nicholas Formio
Anna Whitelock	Stella Herbert

Directed by Nathan Markiewicz

Executive Producer	Ian Grant
Associate Director	George Siena
Stage Manager	Zoë Clarke
Marketing copy and design	Steven Maddocks
Social media marketing	LittleGold Online
Photography	David Sprecher

Stella Europa was produced by Creative Structure Ltd in association with Infinite Space Theatre

Acknowledgements
Alison Burns and Ian Grant of Creative Structure wish to thank:
Andrea Brooks, Zoë Clarke, Nick Hastings, Steven Maddocks, Coralie Prosper, Denise Stephenson, Felicity and James Wren, Dave Wybrow

Act One

Scene One

Brussels, meeting room. The evening after the European parliamentary election in May 2014. In the room: Marine Le Pen is a commanding French politician, on a rising tide of far-right electoral success. She is leader of the French National Front, addressing assembled right-wing MEPs. Geert Wilders is a charismatic Dutch politican, racist and ambitious. Nicholas Formio, British, is in his fifties, well-educated, City background, chipper, combative, hail-fellow-well-met, ambitious. Robertson is a political back-room fixer, of working-class Scottish background. Lambros Fountoulis is a dour Athenian politician of the far-right. Kristina Winberg represents a Swedish right-wing party with a neo-Nazi background.

Le Pen The people have spoken. Our people demand one type of politics: French politics by the French, for the French, with the French. Tonight is a massive rejection of the European Union. What is happening in France signals what will happen in all European countries; the return of the nation. For us, colleagues, we now have the opportunity to make a change, to rediscover the different faces of Europe, to form a conquering alliance of nations against the Brussels euro-élite. Which of you will stand with us?

Wilders Madame, I speak for the Dutch people. We are sick and tired of foreigners who come to our country, they cluster in our towns and spread like cancer cells. They refuse to speak our language, they pollute our streets, they corrupt our young. We are inspired by your sweeping victory in France. My party will stand alongside you. We will cleanse our nations of this filth.

Winberg I am from Sweden. We have same trouble with peoples who do not have Swedish values. We share with you the problem of Muslims invading our society.

Formio We're not going to get allies out of this lot. The press would be all over us. Have you spoken to Grillo?

Robertson We are meeting tomorrow.

Formio Is he mad?

Robertson He's an Italian comedian. But he has seventeen seats, so no, he's not mad. With our twenty-four and his seventeen, we only need a few more odds and sods from different countries to make up our numbers.

Le Pen Nicholas Formio. Ladies and gentlemen, we should congratulate Mr Formio. He has won a fine victory in Great Britain. Mr Formio, will you work with us, join us in our crusade for the new Europe that our people crave?

Formio Madame Le Pen, I thank you for your kind words. In turn, I congratulate you. You have given your French establishment a clear and powerful message.

Le Pen So, Mr Formio, will you join us?

Formio Madame, we have an equal number of seats in the new parliament.

Le Pen Will you join us?

Formio You have refused an alliance with the Jobbik party in Hungary, you will not work with Golden Dawn of Greece. Why do you not ask them to join your group?

Le Pen Mr Formio, this meeting is not a negotiation.

Wilders We don't want the Nazis of Jobbik or Golden Dawn. Or Sweden.

Winberg   You don't call us Nazi.

Wilders   Formio, bring your British democrats into our group. We will be a powerful bloc from northern Europe which will strangle the Euro-élite.

Fountoulis   I am here to save our country.

Wilders   And to kick out the Jews.

Winberg   Jews are bleeding Europe.

Le Pen   I will not have this language in my meeting.

Winberg   This is the language of your father.

Fountoulis   And of your founders, Miss Winberg. You cannot speak.

Le Pen   My father is a patriot, but I lead the National Front of France, not my father.

Robertson   Shall we make our excuses?

Formio   Let it roll a little. I want something for the Daily Mail.

Wilders   Madame, we have important business. Do not engage with these Easterners.

Winberg   You Dutch, you are bad hypocrites. Your Muslims and your Jews are rotting you.

Formio   Madame, you will excuse us. I congratulate you once more on your fine performance in France. Good evening to you, and to all of you, ladies and gentlemen.

Le Pen   We shall speak again tomorrow.

Formio   Madame, I am not free to do so. I cannot associate

	my party with your Nazi friends here. I shall issue a press release to the British media tomorrow. We shall form our own group in the European parliament.
Wilders	You are a fool, Formio.
Le Pen	Let him go. He cannot achieve the numbers.
Formio	I bid you good evening. Robertson, ask that Swedish lady to come and see me after dinner, would you? Let's have a drink.

Exeunt Formio and Robertson

Scene Two

London, university study. On stage are Beatrice, intelligent, hard-working, well brought-up, from middle-class Cornwall; Ally is bright, enthusiastic, full of nervous energy, driven, combative, from working-class Glasgow. Stella is a young professor, Cambridge-educated, upper-middle class, comes from an establishment family.

Stella	Beatrice, you tell us that the Enlightenment in politics is being drowned out by noisy populism. Ally, what do you have for us?
Ally	Well, I mean like Beatrice is just awesome when she comes out with that stuff.
Stella	Well?
Ally	I got something together on the American colonies. But it's not going to be up to Bea's standard.
Stella	I had expected better from your Glasgow degree.
Ally	Well, I'm sorry, but you told us to think about

	Europe, America, the philosophers and that. I'm doing my best. Some of the stuff that, say, Franklin said was like really close to David Hume.

Stella   Example?

Ally   Well, I like Franklin when he goes 'The Constitution only gives people the *right* to pursue happiness. You have to catch it yourself'. I think Hume is all about managing your life yourself, doing something about how it all works.

Stella   Beatrice, let's consider your approach.

Beatrice   The French are difficult. But for a while, in the 1760s, Hume and Adam Smith were intellectual stars in Paris.

Ally   Both from Glasgow University.

Stella   All right, Ally.

Beatrice   They were. But I feel that France inspired them.

Stella   In what way?

Beatrice   Well, Hume introduces Smith to high society in Paris, Smith takes fire and writes 'The Wealth of Nations'. Now I know this is not formal thinking –

Ally   But Bea is right, they were rocking around town, those guys. Paris had the same effect on Franklin. And Scott Fitzgerald. And Henry Miller.

Stella   Ally, please. Beatrice, bring us back. You told us about Enlightenment politics.

Beatrice   Well, I think from the seventeenth century intelligent women and men were rejecting the authority of church and state over thinking and knowledge and exploring a human-centred awareness.

Act One Scene Two

Stella How does this show itself in the politics?

Beatrice I think this was unnerving for the state. And the Church. By the time we get to Hume and Smith we get really practical empiricism, scientific observation of people and if I understand anything of Kant – it's so hard, Professor, it's like banging my head against rock – then he is saying what Hume and Smith are saying – that human beings are highly sensitive to the world around them and in particular to individual people.

Ally Wow, Beatrice.

Stella Go on. This is good. You begin to draw parallels with what's happening now.

Beatrice Well now, we have a kind of jangling noise going on. No one is thinking, they're shouting. Smith doesn't say that you simply agree with the other person, but you both have an interest in a human conversation to try to reach a compromise.

Stella And now – this jangling noise?

Ally It does your head in.

Beatrice I mean ISIS or Ukraine or Gaza or Charlie Hebdo, or, or – on and on – how can anyone imagine that smashing people's homes and massacring schoolchildren is a good idea. Whichever side of these arguments –

Stella That's a mild term –

Beatrice – but whichever side you are on, the other person has become the Other in capital letters. Once that happens, people turn into beasts.

Brief pause

Beatrice It's happening here, the BIP wins by hammering one thing into the heads of voters – the Others are taking your lives away.

Ally But people listen to them. And vote for them.

Stella I'm sorry to say.

Ally But what they say must get home to them.

Beatrice But there's no logic. There's not even facts.

Ally But what he like says, what's his name, Formio, it's making sense to more and more people.

Beatrice There is no sense in what he says.

Ally Not to you. Or to Stella. But to them, to the voters who vote for him, it makes sense.

Stella Why is that? Am I threatened by the people painting my neighbour's house because I don't understand their language?

Beatrice Wouldn't Smith say it's irrational to feel threatened – and maybe – I don't know – irresponsible? It's up to you to sort out what's rational and what the person in front of you needs.

Ally Smith wasn't a house painter who like couldn't get a job.

Stella But he needed to earn, and found a way to do that.

Ally It's different. He like knew people. He was a professor, not a worker.

Stella Am I not a worker?

Ally But I mean, like, labour's different isn't it?

Beatrice I never understand that.

Ally My Dad worked in the shipyards. That's what labour means.

Stella We'll pick this up again. More from you next time, Ally. Good, Beatrice.

Scene Three

London, Notting Hill. On stage: Lady Mary, the consummate establishment social and political hostess, widowed, imperturbable in public, passionate and self-aware; John is a young literary lion, a spendthrift, eloquent, promiscuous, charming and somewhat chaotic.

Lady Mary John, darling, I do like that jacket.

John You're very generous, Lady Mary.

Lady Mary Sit by me. Who is publishing your new poems?

John I think Burning Eye will take them.

Lady Mary Burning Eye? Do we know them? Why have you left Cape?

John I need to be more edgy. Burning Eye are very edgy.

Lady Mary Darling, your work is not for the street. Your poems pull at the heart-strings, not the bootstraps.

John You are kind, Lady Mary. But I have to engage with the world.

Lady Mary As a poet or a priest?

John As both.

Lady Mary I want you to be one of those gorgeous young priests. I long to see your flowing hair drifting over the collar of your vestments.

John My hair is a briar patch; yours pours like a sunlit waterfall.

Lady Mary You are a sweet boy. Your words are runny honey, but you are after my money.

John I am your soul's soldier, not your mercenary. I kneel not for your cold gold, but for one kiss of the jewel of your body.

Lady Mary You will come to me tonight.

Enter Stella

Stella, darling, how lovely to see you.

Stella Hallo, mother. Good afternoon, John.

Lady Mary You know each other?

Stella John is a new visitor to our Humanities department. My students' essays seem to suffer when he has swept in and out.

Lady Mary Oh really. What a reputation.

John Scarcely. Professor Herbert adorns the high table; I footle with words in her shadow.

Lady Mary Do you?

Stella John, you talk nonsense.

John Not so. You write powerfully. You clarify all this noise about Europe – the distance between Brussels and the street.

Lady Mary Oh the street. Stella, this boy says he wants to be – what did you say? – edgy. He wants to wander the streets, and get to know the homeless.

Stella As a poet or a priest?

Lady Mary Exactly, darling. And why not both? I will talk to the Dean, who will make sure he gets plenty of time to write.

John No, I have scarcely begun my studies. I must know the world face to face, I must suffer with the people.

Lady Mary My dear, so vehement. It does you credit and I love your eyebrows when you frown.

Stella Mother, that's unkind. John is right. He must test his vocation.

Lady Mary You are familiar with his beliefs?

John Do you really think Formio speaks for the street?

Stella I distrust him utterly. He speaks at the street. The pint and the slappy grin are effective television. But nobody speaks for Europe.

John What does he want?

Stella Celebrity. He is desperate to be hailed as the 'fox in the hen-house'. He wants to be up the nose of the grown-ups.

Lady Mary Also so vehement, darling.

Stella And he wants money. He wants to be one of those who don't need a wage.

Lady Mary John, darling, I think you said you had an appointment.

John My goodness, I must make my way. Will you please excuse me? Stella, we'll talk more.

Lady Mary Don't be late. And don't forget our arrangement.

John Of course not. It is engraved.

Stella Goodbye, John.

John Goodbye, goodbye.

Exit John

Stella Poor John. I don't think he knows which way to turn. He is brilliant in the lecture hall. If he ever becomes a priest, his sermons will be a wonder.

Lady Mary Stella, darling. Take your hands off him.

Stella What?

Lady Mary I said take your hands off him.

Stella I beg your pardon, mother? I have no interest in John.

Lady Mary You are lying – either to me or to yourself.

Stella Are you mad?

Lady Mary Quite possibly. But that boy pleases me and I won't have you spoiling him for me.

Stella I have no intention of doing anything –

Lady Mary Yes you do. You snare him with your words, and touch him.

Stella He is an occasional colleague.

Lady Mary Then you are an innocent. He worships your status,

Act One Scene Three

and your language. He has a powerful body. Your light touch on his shoulder makes him shudder and you know that.

Stella I most certainly do not know it.

Lady Mary Then your brilliant head is too big for your body.

Stella You seem to know a lot about other people's bodies, mother.

Lady Mary I do, dear. I know John's body better than he does. I know when he kisses my breasts and presses his tongue –

Stella Oh God, mother!

Lady Mary – he is swimming blind, twisting and turning in me.

Stella Oh, please, mother, I don't need to know this.

Lady Mary Don't be prim, dear. Your father was prim.

Pause

Stella My father –

Lady Mary Was a fine man, in his way. Even when he lost his seat, he did not lose heart.

Stella I am trying to make his work stick, so that the students know what true civil liberty is. John brings it alive for them. How long have you known him?

Lady Mary That's none of your business.

Stella How long has this been going on?

Lady Mary What, dear?

Stella You and John – seeing, – sleeping –

Lady Mary We don't get much sleep, darling. Not until breakfast time.

Stella Mother, it's disgusting. He's half your age.

Lady Mary You had better get used to it. Stella, dear, just be careful. Live in your head by all means – you're so good there – but if you have the slightest temptation to touch John – resist it. Don't interfere with him. I'm going to have my bath.

Stella You appal me, mother.

Lady Mary So I see, dear. I will see you tomorrow evening.

Scene Four

Brussels, meeting room. On stage are Formio, Robertson and Winberg.

Formio You made quite an impact in Madame Le Pen's meeting.

Robertson Powerful statements.

Winberg You are not strangers, in Britain, about the difficult situation caused by people from other cultures worming their way into our towns and cities.

Formio What is important is how one says these things. In the British Independence Party we say we welcome skilled workers and their families, from all parts of the world. We ask them, reasonably, to participate in the British way of life.

Winberg In Sweden, we have great problems. These people come into our country, but bring their own country with them also.

Act One Scene Four   17

Robertson   Familiar story.

Winberg   They bring their wives, their mothers, their filthy children, their food, they don't speak our language, they take over complete trades – all of the taxis, the delivery trucks –

Formio   Mrs Winberg, we understand. Your party is small here, but if you join with us we will build a group that will have a strong voice and start to fight back. But we need to move quickly. When we form a group of seven countries, then we have access to a lot of EU money. You will show your voters in Sweden that you have strength and influence.

Brief pause

Winberg   That would be good for our party.

Formio   And would prevent Madame Le Pen from reaching the same pot of money.

Winberg   Why should she not also have this money?

Formio   Her group is a rabble, some of them beyond the worst forms of racism. Have you begun to claim your expenses from the accounts department?

Winberg   I have to find it yet.

Formio   Robertson will take you. Get your claims in early. Make sure you show them the full amount of running your offices, your staff.

Robertson   Our British press are very troubled by the Nazi uniforms some of your party members wear.

Winberg   No-one in Sweden Democrats wears this costume for twenty years.

Robertson   There are some recent photographs.

Winberg In some demonstration young people did dress in historical cultural costume that was not correct for our values.

Robertson Your founder was a Nazi.

Winberg This is finished many years ago.

Robertson We must be sure, Mrs Winberg.

Formio We want you with us. But the British media love a juicy Nazi story, however old.

Winberg In Sweden, we are now the third party. The people vote for us.

Formio Exactly. We understand. Now we will agree a press release to announce that you have joined our group. At the same time we will release a letter from you, renouncing Nazism and the supremacy of the white Nordic people.

Winberg We have not written a letter.

Formio It will be for the best. Join us, and substantial funds will flow from our group into your account. Now, why don't I get my driver to drop you off at your hotel? Robertson, will you give him a call?

Winberg Mr Formio –

Formio Don't mention it, Mrs Winberg. We can all do with funding for our party's cause, I know. It is a pleasure doing business with you. Excuse me. I have to take this call. Robertson will show you the way.

Exeunt Winberg and Robertson

Yes, this is Nicholas Formio. Who is this? Who? Madame Bergeron. Have we met?

Scene Five

University study. On stage are Stella and John.

Stella You have won over the students again. Thank you so much.

John They are very indulgent.

Stella No, you lift their eyes, you free their spirits.

John I loved that boy who asked about 'daring to think, daring to live, daring to love'.

Stella He says things my father used to say.

John I wish I were back at the beginning.

Stella Why? The students adore you.

John It's show. I have no effect on all the ghastly stuff in the world. I'm so poor, I can't do anything the way you can.

Stella Me? John, I teach. You have a vocation, two vocations.

John What are they?

Stella You tell us, over and over. Poetry and the poor.

John Modest poets make no money; penniless philanthropists make no difference. I'm so far from you, Stella.

Stella Father said you have to listen very hard. He told me stories, read to me. Listen to the stories of the world and in the silences between them, listen to yourself.

John I can't hear anything.

Stella You don't give yourself a chance.

John I want to dare. I want to feel and touch. Stella, I admire you.

Stella May I say something?

John Of course.

Stella Don't get sucked into my mother.

Pause

John She is an extraordinary woman.

Stella She may be, but she is not your answer.

John I simply offer to please her.

Stella She is not a simple woman.

John I respond to what she asks of me.

Stella My father loved her very much.

John He was an example.

Stella Step back, John.

John She is hard to resist.

Stella Then you will never hear yourself.

John Will you hear me?

Stella My father was a poet. Away from the House in the Scottish hills he would walk and listen to himself. As I was growing up he would listen to me, very gently. As I was charging about in my head, he would simply listen, not say much, and every now and again would offer a word, a thought. He helped me find my way.

Act One Scene Five

John Stella, would you listen to me?

Stella My mother loved him too. They were so different but they worked, deeply, as husband and wife. Amongst all her noise and the talk and the people, she used to listen to him.

John You understand me.

Stella I don't know if I do.

John I am sure of it.

Stella You must listen to yourself.

John One evening, may I read you some work?

Brief pause

Stella Thank you. I might like that.

John Would you, would you really?

Stella I might.

John When could you come?

Stella Will you resist my mother?

John Oh.

Stella A moment of silence.

John I see.

Brief pause

Stella I might come.

Scene 6

London, university study. On stage are Beatrice and Stella.

Beatrice I'm stumbling around in a mist, banging my shins against rocks. I'm struggling for the words about Adam Smith and the way Europe is today.

Stella I know. We have put Smith into an economics box.

Beatrice He's more important than that.

Stella He is, and you get it. You are right about him and Hume rocking around Paris, as Ally puts it. Now hold that idea, and shift from the 1760s to the 1940s. Less than two hundred years. We're still in Paris. Europe is on its knees after fighting itself almost to the death. It is saved by a blood transfusion from America – debated into existence only a few years after Hume and Smith published their major works. Add in a dash of Thomas Paine. The richness of that – the intuition of human need, the humanity of the other, everyone's basic common interests – deeply infuses Schuman and Monnet. They propose an extraordinary thing – that France and Germany, enemies for centuries, should pool their coal and steel, the raw materials of war. Partners, not competitors. To create a stable society in which people discover themselves and contribute what they can. All the time. Over and over again. It's messy. And it's noble. And we are still here, at peace in Europe. It's an extraordinary achievement. Your Enlightenment philosophers have a lot to answer for.

Pause

Beatrice It's what I want to do.

Stella You can, Beatrice. I'll introduce you to an old friend who has done good work in Brussels. He will tell you how it feels to be at the beating heart of Europe.

Act Two

Scene One

London, Shoreditch. On stage are Jimmy, in his fifties, has ridden many business ventures, some legitimate, others dodgy, knows where to get anything done, and John.

John   Am I not edgy enough?

Jimmy   I mean don't get me wrong, your writing's good, you know. But we've got to push it a bit further. You need to feel it a bit more, get out in the street, round the corner, where it's a bit darker, know what I mean?

John   You mean perversion.

Jimmy   No, my son. I mean colourful. Surprising. Dark/light. Out of the ordinary. You want to be a priest, right?

John   How do you know that?

Jimmy   That's good, being a priest. Some of my best friends – know what I mean? To do that, you have to get to know the people, right?

John   I do. I need to know the people's fears.

Jimmy   That's a nice jacket, John.

John   Thank you.

Jimmy   Some poor bugger would be grateful for that.

John   Yes, I suppose so.

Jimmy   And then the next bugger would like a pair of trousers, and his girl-friend needs a place to stay. And her sister, who's got a two-year-old, can't feed it properly because she's never had a job. And her uncle, who wasn't so nice to her auntie, he hasn't worked for donkey's years, because he won't keep off the bottle. See what I mean, it's a pricey business, easing some of their problems.

John That's why we need to get the politics right.

Jimmy Sod the politics, John. It's the money. Just the money.

John But is it just the money? I need to feel their pain.

Jimmy Yes, my son. You need pain and you need funding. That's why I like you, see? You got the desire, you got the words, you got the connections. I can help you to some funding. Know what I mean?

Brief pause

John How much?

Jimmy Listen, you're in books. I'm in mobile. There are three big things – gambling, education and sex. Gambling I leave to the big boys. I'm too old for education. So that leaves the one subject that everybody wants. I sell twenty thousand downloads a month of some of my titles, and it's growing all the time. You, my son, – because you're a talented writer with a lot of passion, – you, because you got the desire and the vision, – you, because you want to make a splash in your world, – you, sunshine, could have some of that. You could have a lot of that. You could solve a few people's problems. The bishop would be proud of you. And you can help me out with a couple of things.

John You want my work to be more exotic. Jimmy, I can do that.

Jimmy You been to Kiev?

Act Two Scene One   25

John   Kiev? No.

Jimmy They do fantastic work in Kiev. Great development, great code, everything in HTML5, top-end graphics, super-creative and very cheap. And do you know what, there are a couple of girls who run the studio I use, brilliant skills, programming, project management, the lot. And, John, John – they are gorgeous. They are like beautiful racehorses, legs up to their armpits, and the way they move, they're like quite slow and their haunches just roll gently as they get up from their desks and walk about. Know what I mean? I want you to work with them.

John   They sound very talented.

Jimmy They have a problem.

John   What's that?

Jimmy Visas.

John   What do you mean?

Jimmy I want one of them here. Ukraine's not Europe, is it? So she can't just come over. I need your help.

Enter Ally

John   I can't get them visas.

Jimmy Ally. My man. John, you can help with the visas. Ally, listen, sit down, this is John, John Dove – he's a writer, a poet – he's joining the team. John, this is Ally. He's sourcing some great graphic ideas from people he knows in America.

Ally   John, good to meet you. I'm like a real fan of your work.

John   Really, you know my work?

Jimmy	Of course he does. He knows you're getting more bite into your stuff, so we can put out some really classy, high-price material.
Jimmy	Ally, John's going to help us get one of the girls over.
John	I'm not sure I can help.
Ally	I want to show you this like great new company. They're really interested in working with us. They're in the States, they've been going for like a couple of years.
Jimmy	You could have a word with your friends.
John	I have no influence.
Jimmy	But your Lady Mary does, know what I mean?
John	I don't think she does, Jimmy.
Jimmy	And she has your interests at heart. Or somewhere.
Ally	OK look. Look at this.

Pause

John	Oh, my goodness.
Jimmy	I told you he was good, John.
John	Who are these creatures? And who dresses them in that?
Ally	It's all like latex, John. They design it themselves.
John	The masks – and nothing visible, no skin, no flesh except – except –
Jimmy	Yes, John. Except where they are unzipped.

Act Two Scene One

John The staring eyes glare at you, dare you to touch.

Ally And they like really suck you in, John.

Jimmy You can write like that. Look at the way they move, what they do. I want your words to do that. You can do that. Ten grand.

John I can't do that.

Jimmy Ten grand, John. Think how much good you can do with that.

John I'm a published poet.

Jimmy How much do you make from poems, John? Keep yourself in fancy clothes? I'm offering you ten grand, John.

John Ten thousand pounds. For how much text?

Jimmy I don't know, John, couple of thousand words.

John Only two thousand words?

Jimmy Per product, John, per product.

John What?

Jimmy Ten grand per product.

John Oh my God.

Ally It's like beyond crazy. This one gets the most views per month. They're doubling their numbers every quarter. They really want to work with us. We sent them some of your work –

John You've done what?

Ally They like just love it. We're like working on some

	graphics so like we'd have, above the title – John Dove with Rubber Dahlia –
John	What?
Jimmy	Look, I know it's a tricky decision, son. Take this – call it an advance.
John	No, Jimmy. I mean, I'm not sure.
Jimmy	It's all right, John. It's clean. You can do some good with it. Buy yourself something.
Ally	Now John's on board, if we get Tatiana into London we can work really fast.
Jimmy	Talk to Lady Mary for me – she knows the right people.
John	I can't do that, Jimmy. She trusts me.
Jimmy	Nobody gets hurt. All she has to do is have a word, just a word, up at the Foreign Office.
John	We don't have that sort of relationship.
Jimmy	Oh yes you do, John. Where does all that power, that erotic drive them critics talk about, where does that come from, eh?
John	No, Jimmy.
Jimmy	Son, son, this is not very nice. You're a well-brought-up young man. Look in the envelope.
John	You can't buy me, Jimmy.
Ally	John, you have really got the skills we need. The way you like speak to people, the way you create an amazing mood in college.

John College?

Ally Yeah, you give great head to those kids.

John What do you mean?

Ally And Professor Herbert is under your spell too.

John How do you know all this?

Ally She might be interested in this work you're doing.

John No. She mustn't know.

Ally There's no need for her to know.

John No.

Ally So you'll have a word with her mother.

John Give me some time.

Scene Two

London, Notting Hill. On stage are Stella and Beatrice.

Enter Lady Mary and John

Lady Mary Now Beatrice, Stella tells me that you're a philosopher and you want to go into politics. Are you sure?

Beatrice Well, I should like to try. I mean, I am fascinated by philosophy, but I also want to do something worthwhile and practical.

Lady Mary All this doing good. You sound like our poet over there.

Beatrice Oh Mr Dove is wonderful. His lectures are so inspiring.

Lady Mary So I have heard. But politics – why would you want to get mixed up with them? They're not particularly agreeable.

John Lady Mary, what wickedness are you pouring into Beatrice's ear?

Lady Mary Beatrice seems to find you particularly admirable, John.

John I think it would be more helpful if we said a word about Henry, before he comes.

Stella Thank you, John.

Lady Mary Are you two ganging up on me? I'm just trying to get the dear girl to tell me who she is, so that I know what I am dealing with.

Stella Mother, you are not dealing with anything.

John Do you want to go into the Foreign Office?

Beatrice I think I might like to. With Professor Herbert we have been digging into Kant –

Lady Mary Those grand rooms are awfully stuffy, I always find. I'm so sorry, dear, do go on, this is fascinating.

Beatrice – and there's one little piece of Kant where he talks about treating any person, every person, really, not as a means, but as an end. I think he says that we all have obligations to treat each other with justice –

John Oh we do, Beatrice –

Beatrice – and also with what he calls beneficence.

Lady Mary How noble.

Beatrice I didn't mean to sound pompous.

Stella No you didn't. And actually that's the point. There's nothing wrong with nobility, nobility of purpose, nobility of action. Beatrice's work on the BIP scrabbling together a group of far-right MEPs in Brussels shows, rightly –

Enter Henry. Henry is a rising Foreign Office official, Cambridge, establishment family, capable, charming, open to the world.

Lady Mary There you are, Henry. We have been waiting for you.

Henry I'm so sorry, Lady Mary.

Lady Mary Not to worry, darling. And we are secretly rather pleased the Foreign Secretary was otherwise engaged. Now, you know everyone, I think – my daughter Stella –

Henry Lovely to see you again, Stella – far too long –

Lady Mary John Dove.

Henry How do you do? I am familiar with your work, of course.

John Really? I'm delighted.

Lady Mary You may not have met Beatrice – Beatrice –

Beatrice Tremain.

Lady Mary Of course, Beatrice Tremain.

Henry Miss Tremain, how do you do?

Beatrice Very well, thank you.

Stella Beatrice is one of my students. We were just talking about the BIP in Europe. I am appalled at the company they keep.

Henry I think they'll succeed.

Stella It's infuriating. Formio is simply making it up. He offers nothing. Beatrice is very interested in the Foreign Office and I hope you might be able to give her a flavour.

Henry Delighted, if I can.

John *(to Lady Mary)* You must ask him.

Lady Mary Be quiet. He's only just arrived. I don't know if I can do it.

John You must. I have promised that you will.

Lady Mary There is no 'must'.

John For me, there is.

Lady Mary I will not be bullied.

John You promised me last night.

Henry Everyone wants the glamorous postings, of course, Paris, Washington, but there is interesting, knotty work to be done everywhere.

Beatrice Where have you been?

Henry A year in Brussels with our trade delegation then two main postings so far – New Delhi and Cairo.

Beatrice That's so exciting.

Henry And then a lot of commuting from Kentish Town to the Office – not so much fun.

Stella	And are you doing good?
Henry	I hope so.
Stella	Really?
Henry	Impossible to know. Possibly in our work in the EU.
Stella	I don't believe it. We are dreadful in Europe.
Henry	It's awful in the headlines. But our people in Brussels are working every day with all our partners, making the EU work, getting the single-market working, free movement of people across what used to be guarded national borders, particularly the old Iron Curtain.
Beatrice	That's fascinating.
Henry	It's an enormous achievement. It has its ups and downs, but ultimately all citizens benefit hugely.
Lady Mary	Look at you all, like diplomats plotting the downfall of a potentate.
Henry	Those days are in the history books, Lady Mary.
Lady Mary	Has he convinced you to become an Ambassador, Beatrice?
Beatrice	I would love to hear more.
Lady Mary	Well, you must be patient for a while. I would like a quiet word with our guest, for a few moments.
Stella	John, come and tell us what you are working on.
Beatrice	Professor Herbert told me you have something new coming.

Stella When there is an article about you I always click the link. You are becoming more racy.

John I don't know about that.

Stella I should look out for my job. Particularly if you are going to introduce gritty erotic verse into your lectures.

Lady Mary It's a simple little thing, Henry. It's just a colleague of John's who is helping with his new collection, an academic, I think. God knows what there is in Ukraine. But it would be so helpful, if you could have a word, to ease his passage into the country.

Henry Visas are not my department.

Lady Mary No dear, you are much too senior, I know.

Henry It may be simple. I did some work in Brussels with Ukraine. If I remember correctly, people with biometric passports don't need visas. Let me have a word.

Lady Mary Henry, you are such a sweet boy. Your mother says she scarcely sees you. What do you think of Beatrice?

Stella Formio simply enrages me. His politics is gross. He is like a turkey-cock in Strasbourg. He is incredibly rude to the Commissioners and to the President, tells them they are incompetent nobodies. He puffs himself up as the saviour of the nation state and the rights of the individual.

John Ghastly, Stella, I agree.

Stella I try to encourage my students to discover where our social agreements come from, how the Enlightenment is at the root of modern German thought, French thought. A dwarf like Formio plasters himself all over the English people, all beer and fags and the Fifties. The main parties are so frightened of Europe, and he just scoops up the votes. Are we all so stupid?

Lady Mary My daughter can become rather emotional.

Henry She is her father's daughter. And she has a point. The PM makes it easy for Formio.

Lady Mary Stella, dear, you have become vehement again.

Stella I'm not vehement, mother, I'm furious. John thinks I should be furious more publicly.

Lady Mary John, take your arm from Stella's waist. Henry, I wonder if you might not take Stella and Beatrice around the corner to that nice little restaurant we go to. Stella sounds hungry to me.

Stella I'm sorry to make such a fuss. It would be fun. We can bore Beatrice with tales of Cambridge long ago.

Beatrice I don't want to intrude –

Henry Not at all, I want to hear much more about your plans. Do join us.

Lady Mary You take the girls off. I have some business to attend to with John.

Stella John, thank you for putting up with me on my hobby-horse.

John I think you should do it.

Beatrice Thank you so much for inviting me, Lady Mary.

Lady Mary You're very welcome, dear. I am sure we shall meet again soon.

Henry Good night, Lady Mary.

Lady Mary Good night, dear. Please give my love to your mother.

Stella Good night, mother.

Lady Mary Off you go.

Exeunt Stella, Beatrice, Henry

I have sorted it out for you.

John You are an angel.

Lady Mary I am.

John Let me enfold you.

Lady Mary No. Listen to me. Does your academic have a new passport?

John My what?

Lady Mary The researcher from Kiev. If he has a recent passport – a biometric passport – then he does not need a visa. I assume he is young.

John I think she is quite young, yes.

Lady Mary She? You didn't say a girl. How do you know her?

John She is more technical than academic.

Lady Mary You are being irritating and obscure. I do not want to waste my time buttering up Henry Anscombe, if you can't be straight with me about who this person is.

John Was I not straight with you last night?

Lady Mary Don't be childish. If it is so important that you get this woman to London, then tell me who she is.

John She is a graphic designer of computer games with unique expertise. She is going to visualise some of my new work and create a sensation with my new material.

Lady Mary Oh really. I don't wish to be used. I will not be taken for granted.

John My darling, I shall take you as you lie like Venus in your bower. I shall take you as you crawl across your magical carpets.

Lady Mary You disgust me.

John Yes, I do, I do.

Lady Mary Leave Stella alone.

John I am only yours. Come, I will show you how I am only yours.

Lady Mary I am going to have a bath. Come to my room in an hour.

John That is beyond eternity.

Lady Mary Help yourself to a drink.

Scene Three

The stage is split:
BBC broadcasting studio. Laura is a bright, savvy, confident TV current affairs journalist, interviewing Formio.
London, university study: Stella, Beatrice and Ally are watching the broadcast.

Laura Mr Formio. You have formed the Europe of Freedom and Democracy Group, you have enough MEPs to qualify for up to 22 million euros of funding as a political group in Strasbourg.

Formio You ask the mass of people who voted for us in constituencies up and down the country, who are having a hard time, who see the great gap opening up between the super-wealthy and the rest, who struggle to find decent work and when they do their wages slip behind the costs of living year after year, you ask them whether being part of a political union with an open door to 450 million people who have the right to come to Britain, take British jobs, occupy British homes, is the way forward.

Laura Many people from Britain make a virtue of free movement within Europe, in order to live and work in another European country.

Formio It's one thing to retire to Spain and spend your pension in the sunshine. It's quite another thing when you are trying to feed your wife and two kids on a modest wage in a small house in England and next door you have a houseful of Romanians who are coming and going at all hours, taking over whole sectors of trades and businesses where formerly the work was there for British people, creating noise and rubbish in the streets.

Laura That is a caricature of British society.

Act Two Scene Three   39

Formio Who is Britain run by? A tiny group of people who all went to the same schools, all went to Oxbridge, all did the same degrees and marry each other's sisters. That's the caricature of how a democracy should be run, yet that's what we've got.

Ally He's really smart.

Laura I put it to you that the Britain you portray no longer exists, if in fact it ever did.

Stella (*speaks over Laura*) He is. His people give him problems.

Formio I'm talking about society now. Our people are out on the street, in the community, making sensible arguments about issues that voters worry about. And people vote for them.

Stella Because no-one is saying anything else.

Laura Our society now, in Britain, is made up of people from many different backgrounds, religions, countries. The BIP's rhetoric stirs up feelings of 'Us' and 'Them', making people anxious for their futures. One of your candidates said she 'wants to send the whole lot back'.

Formio I have been very clear with the British people. I will not rest until we get Britain out of Europe. Seventy-five per cent of our laws in Britain now come from Brussels.

Stella That's such nonsense.

Formio Our country is changing because of the waves of people who come from the Muslim countries and from Eastern Europe, and people don't like it.

Laura There are no waves – the numbers don't say that.

Formio We won the European election. In the General Election, we will return political power where it belongs – to the local people in the cities, the towns, the villages, we'll save ourselves an enormous amount of money and open up our opportunities to the rest of the world, where we made our greatest fortunes when we ruled ourselves.

Stella Turn it off. I can't stand his voice. The prospect of him leading a party in parliament is terrifying.

Ally But it's possible.

Beatrice He generates huge coverage.

Ally Recognition is like so powerful. If he's smart, he will keep that going full bore so that he gets a national TV debate with the leaders of the other parties.

Stella So much money goes to these groups. Most of it will find its way into the pockets of the MEPs.

Beatrice You're very angry.

Stella Yes I am. I am furious. It takes a huge amount of time and effort for people to find the goodwill, the understanding and the compromises to get where Europe is today. Formio is not stupid, he knows this. He knows he can't be top dog but he wants people to watch him, cheer him on, make him feel like a player.

Ally And the system has let him. He's like so high profile because he's won enough votes to get his party into Strasbourg and his group into the money.

Stella It's dangerous, Ally. The nonsensical drivel about Europe in the British media gives Formio all the room in the world. His easy solution – everyone

	out, back to where we were, 'two world wars and one World Cup' – it's so easy to play it up if no-one is presenting the opposite case.
Ally	Why don't you do it?
Stella	Well, I try to, in my teaching and our discussions.
Ally	I mean, like, in public.
Stella	What do you mean?
Ally	I mean you should stand in the election.
Stella	Stand for parliament?
Ally	Against Formio. You are like so passionate about Europe. You can't stand him. Like go for it.

Brief pause

Stella	You're mad, Ally. I'm not a politician.
Ally	So much the better.
Beatrice	That would be amazing. You would have huge support if you stood up to him. All of your students would be out on the street.
Ally	And we could build a proper like crowd-sourced campaign, like Obama's, Twitter, really like use social media where it should be used.
Stella	No, you're getting carried away.
Beatrice	No he's right. It would turn all our thinking into political action in such a brilliant way.
Ally	Go like head to head with Formio, win or lose, the philosophy department here will not be able to like move for applicants. You will be all over the media.

Stella   It sounds appalling.

Ally   Formio is appalling. I mean, like, everything you have taught us, the humanity of Hume and Smith, reason and sympathy, making space for the other man or woman, you know, understanding the interests of the individual, not throwing them out – everything that Formio gets so wrong – this is like your big moment, your time.

Stella   Ally, you astonish me.

Scene Four

London, Shoreditch. On stage are Jimmy, John and Ally.

Jimmy   You owe me two things. Now. The words for the videos. And the visa for the Ukrainian girl.

Ally   Here's like the opening sequence I dummied up.

John   Oh Christ. Those bodies. Encased and… and… exposed. Vacant eyes. And my name. God, where are you putting my name? You can't.

Ally   John, John, this is like just the mock-up. Don't worry. But this is what they're buying. I mean, you see the quality. And they're buying you.

Jimmy   We need the first script in forty-eight hours.

John   So soon.

Jimmy   Sooner. And the visa for the girl.

John   I have done that. If she has the right passport, she doesn't need a visa.

Jimmy   She needs the passport.

Act Two Scene Four   43

                get her a passport.

                do the passport. Friend of mine round the
                er. You need to get it to the girl.

John   I can't take it to Ukraine – you said it's a war zone.

Jimmy   You'll need to find a friend.

John   What friend?

Ally   John, look how this Dahlia sequence unfolds. Do you see what she's like doing to her?

John   Oh my God. No, don't turn it off.

Ally   I'll email it to you.

Jimmy   You know your diplomatic people.

Ally   Watch the whole thing when you get home.

John   Forty-eight hours. Two thousand words.

Jimmy   Diplomatic bag. Maybe Henry Anscombe.

Ally   Imagine you are like with those girls, watching them, touching them.

John   Yes.

Ally   Or one of them is someone you really fancy. I mean maybe Lady Mary.

John   I'm not sure she's that shape.

Jimmy   Or Laura Anscombe. She travels.

John   In a latex skin. Stella.

Ally   Oh John. Stella.

John No, I don't mean Stella.

Ally Oh I think you do.

Jimmy Whatever, John, whatever helps you to deliver. Text and passport. A friend of mine will come over to your place to help you concentrate. Here. Here's your next advance – double. Buy something nice for the bishop.

Scene Five

London, Notting Hill. On stage are Lady Mary, Laura and Henry.

Lady Mary Your interview with Mr Formio was quite a coup, darling.

Laura I was lucky to pin him down.

Lady Mary Well, your mother was very proud of you. As she is of both of you. I expect you know, Henry, that your mother is much taken by Beatrice.

Laura Henry is much taken by Beatrice, aren't you dear brother?

Henry I confess, I confess. My sister and Beatrice have ganged up on me.

Lady Mary Quite right too. The sooner you propose to the dear girl and we can get the wedding into our diaries, the more convenient it will be for all of us.

Henry Am I to propose to Beatrice, book church, minister, reception and honeymoon in order to get it all done before the General Election?

Lady Mary That would suit very well, dear.

Laura Even Beatrice might find that a bit of a gallop. She will spend all day and night working for Stella, if she decides to stand.

Lady Mary Stand?

Laura Don't you know?

Lady Mary No, dear, I don't think I do. Know what?

Laura That Stella is standing against Formio in the General Election.

Lady Mary Is she indeed? She hasn't mentioned it.

Laura I think she scarcely knows herself. Beatrice said they talked long into the night, Stella and Beatrice and that energetic boy she teaches.

Henry Ally's quite a driver apparently. They are much taken by John Dove's mix of poetry, politics and the priesthood. I'm not sure that Stella is quite aware of the effect he has on them.

Lady Mary Isn't she? Henry, warn her to be careful of him.

Laura When he heard I was flying to Kiev, he became very excited.

Lady Mary Tell her that she should discuss him with her faculty – I don't think he helps the university's reputation.

Henry I'm not sure he's actually dangerous. What's on in Kiev?

Laura Poroshenko. Wants to do an interview late tomorrow. Dove said he had a lead for me.

Henry Dove? What lead?

Laura Business colleagues.

Henry What's Poroshenko's line?

Laura Not sure yet. We're expecting something tonight then briefing as we arrive.

Lady Mary It would be rather nice for Stella to stand in her father's old constituency. Who's the chairman now?

Laura She wants to fight Formio.

Lady Mary Better to find an agreeable seat and do that in the House, surely.

Henry I think the fight is Stella's point.

Lady Mary She certainly gets very worked up about him.

Laura Your husband's principles run very deep in her.

Lady Mary Your father and he were such good friends. They would have had fun together in retirement.

Henry This won't be fun. Stella will take a battering if she stands against Formio.

Lady Mary We have had some campaigns in this household. I hadn't expected another one. I'm surprised Stella wants to stand, but do you know, I might be quite excited.

Scene Six

London, university study. On stage are Ally, Stella and Beatrice.

Ally Stella. This is like the real moment.

Stella I don't know. I'm an academic, I research, I teach. I don't battle in public.

Ally   Let it come through. You have this opportunity now to like put all you teach and believe into practice. Formio is getting momentum, he is choosing the seats the BIP will fight, he is announcing where he is going to stand. You have to fight him.

Stella   Ally, what is it to you?

Beatrice   It's the same for Ally as it is for me. We believe in you.

Ally   It's great for me. My grades will like go through the roof – theory in the real world. I can get the whole Kickstarter thing moving the moment you announce. We will raise good, clean money. We can get a terrific social media campaign going which will fox Formio.

Stella   He has the whole of the right-wing press.

Ally   They think they're in the online game, but they have no idea. We will roll them over.

Beatrice   Henry thinks you should stand.

Stella   You've talked about it?

Ally   John is like really fired up. He will be really fantastic in public.

Stella   You've talked to him?

Ally   Oh sure. He's like on fire. He really fancies you, by the way.

Stella   What?

Ally   But it won't get in the way. I'll see to it.

Scene Seven

BIP committee rooms. Celia is a middle-class ardent amateur politician, always pleased to help, although a touch behind the times. Jack is a gruff man-of-the-people political party activist. Ted is a middle-aged, lower middle-class amateur politician. Angela is a capable political manager, doesn't suffer fools.

Enter Formio.

Celia Ladies and gentlemen, Mr Nicholas Formio.

Formio Oh, really, don't be daft. Please sit down everyone, sit down. We're not in the Tory party here. Now thank you all for coming.

Celia No thank you, Nick. Your bravery in the European parliament, standing up for Britain, criticising the stitch-up of office holders and so on, it really shows them we mean business.

Jack It's a different game, here. No-one cares how rude you are to the European crowd, we'll have to play a different game here.

Ted We smacked 'em hard in Strasbourg. You took it to 'em. We beat Le Pen out of the money, and now you're going for the EU bosses.

Jack But, I'm saying, that's not going to work here.

Formio Well, now look, we have to fight the enemy in front of us. But we all have to stick to the same line. I don't want any of the nonsense we had at our conference and in Thurrock. It's a bloody nuisance on a big news day when someone loses the plot and I have to spend all my time clearing up the mess.

Celia You're right Nick. And your strong leadership got us through those tricky moments.

Angela Yes, Celia. Now to business: our manifesto is clear, simple and strong. You have all had a chance to read it.

Ted We're not strong enough on immigration. 'Send 'em home', that's what I get on the doorstep, time and time again.

Formio I know. When we hear it on the doorstep, we agree. When we meet soft Tories we have to talk economics. We have to say the problem is the impact of foreigners on unskilled British workers.

Ted Not just unskilled. Our boys and girls can't get jobs because of all them who get the jobs and houses before us.

Celia My granddaughter's school is full of them. The Chinese are very bright, you know.

Angela Can we stick to one section of the manifesto at a time, please? We deal with schools later.

Formio When we're talking to a working-class housewife in a Labour home, it's the problems with housing because foreign workers get preference on the lists – there's definitely a vote there for us.

Jack The more of them there are, the more they claim.

Angela The point is not unemployment benefit.

Ted Yes, it is. They come over here and live on the dole. You see 'em all over, gypsies, Greeks, Arabs, I don't know what. They come over by the boatload from Africa. There'd be a hell of a lot more if half of 'em didn't get washed away on the way over.

Angela That's not for our manifesto.

Ted Well, it bloody well should be. We're a soft touch.

You don't see boatloads of people going the other way, do you, struggling to get to Africa? Why's that, I wonder?

Formio Angela, just summarise the manifesto points on this one, will you?

Angela One, the country is full; two, open-door immigration from Europe is swamping our services and housing; three, mass immigration from former communist countries with low wage expectations is damaging the prospects of British workers; four, we are powerless to control this while we are in the EU.

Formio That's it in a nutshell. Now, in the latest polls we're in third place, leading the Greens and Lib Dems by about eight points. We are going to be the kingmakers. The Lib Dems are finished but we should remember how Paddy Ashdown built them up by getting them to focus on a small number of constituencies. That's our job now. We made huge gains at the local and European elections. Do not forget that, my friends. We won in Europe.

Jack Nick, nobody cares about that here.

Formio They don't care about being in. They are desperate to get out.

Angela That's section five of the manifesto.

Celia What are sections two, three and four?

Angela Health, education and tax.

Jack I didn't see those.

Angela We haven't drafted them yet.

Formio We'll look at those shortly. They're fairly straightforward. But the point we have to make about Europe is that we are the only party that is having no nonsense – complete withdrawal, now, is our position.

Jack What about our money?

Angela What's your point?

Jack We make a very good living out of the EU. Nick created a steady flow of funds into our accounts by winning the fight against Le Pen. We're not just going to chuck that away.

Formio There's plenty more where that came from.

Scene Eight

University study. Onstage are John, Stella.

John I haven't seen her.

Stella It's right. Mother will know that.

John We're bound to meet.

Stella She'll forgive you. She will be harder with me.

John But she'll support you against Formio.

Stella Of course she will. She loves election campaigns. She's rather good at them.

John You are so brave.

Stella I'm terrified. But I see the effect you have on our students. They get it. They get that we must look into people's eyes and listen. People are Us, not the Other. They may or may not know this is Enlightenment thought. But when you speak your finest lines to them and they hear your voice resonate around the hall, around them, through them, they are uplifted, John. I feel it. I am uplifted, too.

John Stella, Stella. I am not worth this.

Stella I need you. I need you by my side.

John I am not worthy.

Stella When I stand up to fight, in public, I must know that you are close.

John I didn't believe you would do this.

Stella You opened my eyes.

John I saw your fire.

Pause

Stella To be human is to share and dare and feed the fire in each other.

John Your fire consumes me.

Stella Your fire burns in me.

John Your flames are my light.

Stella Your light shines through me.

John Your words are my song.

Stella As your words sing through me. Let them carry me up, John, and help me fight this mindless loathing that whips up the filth from the streets. Bring out our young. Formio stands in our light.

Act Three

Scene One

London. Kentish Town. On stage are Laura and John.

Laura   I appreciate the lead, John.

John   The fellow who runs the business is well connected. Here's his card. It's a graphic design business – he does a lot of online stuff and radical political pamphlets, posters and such like. He has good contacts.

Laura   That's great, John, thanks. I will try to call him. I must run.

John   Could you do me a small favour, Laura?

Laura   My taxi's here.

John   Could you just drop this in at his office in Kiev? Or if you can't, just put it in a cab.

Laura   Sure. Yes, yes, I'm coming down. What is it, John?

John   Just some material for the designers.

Laura   Can't you send it?

John   If you could, Laura, it would be so helpful.

Laura   Give it to me, I'm going to miss the plane.

Scene Two

London, Notting Hill. On stage are Henry and Lady Mary.

Henry I'm neutral, publicly, of course.

Lady Mary Do you think she's up to it?

Henry If she can stand the media pressure.

Lady Mary She's strong-willed. And very bright, of course. But she's an academic, she's not been blooded.

Henry It's a big risk.

Lady Mary She saw plenty of campaigns when her father was alive.

Henry And was active, very active in the last one he fought.

Lady Mary He would have approved, whole-heartedly. She has his idealism.

Henry And his courage, if I may say so.

Lady Mary You are a dear boy, Henry. You were a good friend to her at Cambridge.

Henry What she believed in then still burns. This may be her moment.

Lady Mary What do you think of Formio?

Henry He's a very tough nut. He's on a run, he gets the coverage, the government is very scared of losing the Tory right to him. According to the polls he is well ahead of the Lib Dems who are now losing to the Greens. Stella will have a mountain to climb.

Lady Mary Does she have the strength?

Henry She probably does, but of course no direct experience. She will need an extremely good campaign manager. Formio will use every means to strike at her weaknesses.

Lady Mary Are you on her side?

Henry His behaviour is appalling in Strasbourg. He is a terrible advertisement for Britain, and one can see members from other countries just close their eyes or leave the chamber when he speaks. Behind the scenes I shall do everything I can.

Lady Mary Who can manage the campaign?

Henry I don't know. He or she will need to be an exceptional operator. I will talk to one or two people.

Lady Mary Bless you, dear boy.

Scene Three

London, Shoreditch. Tatiana is warm-hearted, cold-blooded, very attractive and very efficient. She is on stage with Jimmy, Ally and John. / Split stage – also BBC studio – Laura is interviewing Stella.

Ally Tatiana, this is democracy in action, Stella announcing that she is going to stand for parliament. Goes back hundreds of years.

Jimmy Come over here and sit by me.

Laura Professor Herbert, you have been selected by the Green Party as their parliamentary candidate in South Thanet. You are an academic, a philosopher, unknown in politics. Isn't this simply a quixotic tilt at Nicholas Formio?

John   Oh come on, Laura, that's hard to start with.

Stella   Not at all, we have the clearest and simplest policies of all the parties.

Tatiana   She is the woman in Kiev. She came with passport.

John   You must never say that.

Stella   Three key pledges – fighting austerity, promoting public ownership and making the transition from fossil fuels.

Tatiana   Why? She was very kind, to come so far.

Stella   And as well as its strong domestic policies, the Green Party is very clear on its stance in Europe.

Ally   John, it's great Tatiana's here, eh? She did some fantastic work in the studio today.

Jimmy   I knew you'd come through, John. Great script, edgy, sophisticated.

Stella   No, the Green Party have a very consistent record, a strong core of support in South Thanet.

Laura   But the Greens have never even come close, this is your personal battle against Nicholas Formio. How will that benefit the constituents of South Thanet?

John   Stella, watch your step.

Ally   Was it Stella you had in mind, when you were doing the voiceover, John?

John   No it was not Stella. Listen, I want to hear her.

Stella   There is no intelligent opposition to the British Independence Party in this country. The Tories are terrified, their new candidate in South Thanet was even a member of the BIP not long ago. The Labour Party is horribly ambiguous on immigration. I am standing because the BIP is a dangerous sham. It has no policies to put forward on major issues and its position on immigration is a vicious slur on people who wish to come to the UK to make a life here.

John She is magnificent.

Ally She is. You wouldn't want to cause her any problems, John, would you?

Laura With respect, Professor Herbert, you seem to confuse the issues of immigration – people come from many countries outside Europe as well as from the European Union – with the question of EU membership. Nicholas Formio is very clear on both.

Stella The people of South Thanet will not be bounced into the racist position of the BIP. Most people who come to work in Britain are hard-working tradespeople who pay their taxes –

Ally Tradespeople. I'm not sure that Stella is like in touch with the 'tradespeople' – not in the social bubble she lives in.

John She meets people from every background – I mean look at you.

Ally What do you mean, look at me? I have roots, my friend, I come from the working people of Glasgow. Stella has no idea about Glasgow, she thinks we like come from the sticks.

John She does not.

Ally You're just the same as she is. All your fucking nonsense about meeting the people on the street.

Jimmy Now lads, come on, now.

Ally You're one of them up to your neck, my friend. Up to your neck in Stella's mother. Probably just as far in to posh Laura Anscombe and there they are, pretending to have like a tough debate on Newsnight, then they'll all go off for drinks with smart brother Henry. Who's fucking marrying Beatrice.

Jimmy Now then Ally.

John Just shut up, you little punk. Stella should just drop you.

Stella Laura, Europe is the source of our peace and security. Since the Second World War people have worked slowly, with great difficulty, but with patience, skill and intelligent compromise – with diplomacy, which is a great British skill – Europe has grown ever more safe, ever more secure – welcoming more people into its embrace –

Tatiana She is a good woman. In Kiev, we fight for Europe, too.

Jimmy Turn off the telly.

Ally Tatiana, when are we sending the complete files of the first product to LA?

Tatiana We could send in two days, maybe three days.

Ally We wouldn't want the launch of the Rubber Dahlia/John Dove erotic video series to clash with your first election speech in support of Stella, would we?

John You said it was only on Pay-TV in hotels. Nothing about a launch.

Jimmy HNC-TV are keen to get more material for

Act Three Scene Three

syndication. And Tatiana's here and working. All thanks to you, John.

Ally And Laura. What would the BBC have to say about Laura Anscombe trafficking passports to Kiev?

Jimmy We need you working for us.

John I am.

Ally Like all the time.

John But the campaign's just beginning. Stella needs me.

Jimmy We need you, full time, focused, working here. Know what I mean?

John You said yourself, the publicity is good.

Ally The right publicity, John, the right publicity.

John What are you saying?

Ally I could make two calls, John. One to 'The Sun on Sunday', telling them about the launch of the first Rubber Dahlia/John Dove lesbian latex video; and one to the Home Office, mentioning Laura's little bit of passport smuggling in Kiev. Your name will come up in both calls. Stella wouldn't like that.

John No. No. You can't do that. You mustn't do that. You'll wreck it, you'll wreck everything.

Ally Just stay where you are. Tatiana, get him a drink, will you? Cheer him up a bit. And when she has done that, you had better get back to work, John. Do you see?

Act Four

Scene One

London, Notting Hill. On stage are Lady Mary, Stella, Henry and Ally.

Henry We have to play up your passion and conviction. The mix of Formio and your status will get all the media coverage we can ask for.

Lady Mary May I make a comment, dear?

Stella Yes, mother.

Lady Mary That first interview with Laura – I know it was the first – she was direct but not hostile.

Ally She was quite tough.

Henry They will get much tougher.

Lady Mary Quite. I think you have to come across more naturally, less professorial.

Beatrice You dealt with the questions very well.

Lady Mary She did, dear, but as Henry says they are going to get much tougher. These are not seminars – we are going into battle. You do remind me of your father. He was often too polite in battle.

Stella He won his seat.

Henry Ally, what have the Greens got in the way of social media presence?

Ally Not much. Like a very wordy amateur website.

Henry We need full power on that.

Act Four Scene Two   61

Beatrice We'll be ready in a few days. We'll need a constant stream of content, comment. The BIP are good at it – they overtook most of the other parties after the European elections.

Ally We need good images and video.

Lady Mary Where is John? We need his voice.

Ally Leave that to me.

Henry He's not critical. Stella, we need to leave. Your schedule is tight.

Scene Two

BIP office. On stage are Formio and Robertson.

Formio Who is she?

Robertson A philosophy professor.

Formio Well, that shouldn't be too difficult.

Robertson The latest poll has us on twenty-five percent, the Greens on three percent.

Formio What did they get last time?

Robertson Didn't stand.

Formio They're dead in the water – not worth worrying about.

Robertson We should be careful about Stella Herbert. She is very well-connected. Her father was highly respected in the House.

Formio But she's got nothing to do with South Thanet.

Robertson She will bring big guns. The Greens have asked their first candidate to stand aside for her.

Formio What does he say about that?

Robertson He was miffed at first, but has come round to the idea.

Formio Bearing a grudge?

Robertson Possibly. We'll see.

Formio Have we got anything else?

Robertson She's a top academic. Published on the liberties of the individual and civil society –

Formio Gets that from her father –

Robertson Passionate about European civilization.

Formio Well, end of story. No-one cares about Europe.

Robertson She'll come after you though.

Formio See what else you can find. I mean I'm not worried. We had the biggest majority anywhere in the South East here in the Euros. We're going after the Tories here, but we don't want to be tripped up.

Scene Three

London, university common room. On stage are Ally and Beatrice.

Beatrice Henry isn't like that.

Ally Is he not? That's good. I wouldn't want you to be, you know, disappointed.

Act Four Scene Three 63

Beatrice You are sweet, Ally.

Ally I just want you to be a bit careful.

Beatrice I have my eyes open.

Ally You know you can talk to me.

Brief pause

Ally Do you see much of his sister?

Beatrice Not much. She's always flying off.

Ally I just like heard something, the other day.

Beatrice What did you hear?

Ally I guess it's nothing.

Beatrice What?

Ally No, it doesn't matter.

Beatrice No, what?

Pause

Ally Well, look, don't say anything.

Beatrice What are you talking about?

Ally Someone told me that Laura had been, like, carrying passports to people.

Beatrice Passports?

Ally Out of the country.

Beatrice Where?

Ally Eastern Europe.

Beatrice Why on earth would she do that?

Ally It sounds like really crazy.

Beatrice That can't be true. It's nonsense. I can't believe it.

Ally I'm sure it's just a rubbish rumour.

Beatrice Who told you?

Ally I just overheard it.

Beatrice Do you think I should tell Henry?

Ally Oh, maybe I wouldn't bother with that.

Beatrice But I think he should know.

Ally I'm sure it's just nonsense.

Beatrice I think I should.

Ally It's up to you.

Scene Four

London, Shoreditch. On stage are John and Jimmy.

John I can't go on with this.

Jimmy You can. I've paid you.

John There are only so many ways of expressing erotic desire in latex with holes in.

Jimmy Say it again. The punters are looking at the girls.

John	I'm up to schedule. Stella's people are asking where I am. I've run out of answers.
Jimmy	You'll have to keep making them up, won't you, son? Do you want to me to call Stella and tell her where your money is coming from?
John	Oh God, no. No. No, but I have to go to a meeting, otherwise they will come looking.

Pause

Jimmy	Ally fancies Beatrice.
John	So what? She's virtually engaged to Henry.
Jimmy	Doesn't stop him fancying her, does it? He's a determined little sod. He'll put a spoke in Mr Henry Anscombe's wheels.
John	He's a bastard. You're both bastards.
Jimmy	Yeah. So what are you going to do?
John	You're murdering bastards. You're killing me. Why are you doing this to me?
Jimmy	It's business, John. Nothing personal, son. Know what I mean?

Scene Five

London, Notting Hill. On stage are Stella, Beatrice and Henry.

Henry	This information –
Stella	We don't know it's true.
Henry	– doesn't leave this room.

Beatrice   But Ally's out there. I don't know who else he's told.

Henry   We have to shut it down.

Stella   Laura didn't know.

Henry   That makes it worse. We have to cancel her interview with John Dove.

Beatrice   I've set it all up. There is a buzz going. It will look bad.

Henry   I don't care. We can't have MY SISTER interviewing Dove with this thing smelling like a drain.

Stella   We don't know yet.

Henry   We can't afford not to know. Dove's been fucking stupid. Where is he now? Why isn't Ally here?

Beatrice   I've called Ally. He said he's on his way.

Henry   Beatrice, tell me again exactly what Ally said.

Beatrice   I can't remember exactly, but he said he had overheard a conversation –

Henry   Where?

Beatrice   He didn't say.

Henry   Did he say 'overheard' or that someone had told him?

Beatrice   Yes. Or no. Actually I think he said both.

Henry   And he said Laura had delivered some passports in Kiev?

Beatrice Yes.

Henry And he didn't say to whom.

Beatrice No.

Henry It's very thin but it's totally toxic – toxic to Laura, toxic to Stella –

Stella And to you, Henry.

Henry It smells to high heaven. What are you thinking?

Stella We may need to fire Ally. Quickly.

Scene Six

BIP office. On stage is Ally.

Ally Can I talk to Mr Formio?

Scene Seven

London, Notting Hill. On stage are Henry, Ally and John.

Ally You're so fucking stupid.

Henry Ally, that's enough. I know it's disappointing.

Ally You have no idea.

John Stella and I have decided.

Ally You're fucking dead.

Henry Ally. Enough. I must ask you to leave.

Pause

Ally Rubber Dahlia, Mr Professional Politico.

John Get out.

Ally Rubber Dahlia, starring John hard-core Dove.

John Don't do this to her.

Henry What are you –

Ally The hottest latex lesbian sex.

John You little bastard. Henry, get him out. Get him out now.

Ally You're in like so fucking pieces.

Henry Get a grip on yourself.

Ally You had better, like, tell him, you hot-shit dirty poet priest. Because 'The Sun on Sunday' is waiting for you.

Exit Ally. Pause.

Henry And?

Pause

And? What is 'The Sun on Sunday' waiting for?

John We're finished. It's the worst thing I've ever done. I will write to Stella. She'll never see me again.

Henry What are they waiting for?

John I've been exploring some themes in my writing, developing a harder edge to my lyrical verse. Oh God, it's all gone so horribly wrong. I wanted to

Act Four Scene Seven   69

	help, to make some money to contribute –
Henry	What has Ally got?
John	I was drowning – against my will – I hated it – extraordinary scenes, girls doing – everything – very slowly – I've never seen –
Henry	You're doing hard-core porn. And speaking for Stella in public. What are you thinking? What on earth are you thinking? Who is the producer? Is any of the material out?
John	Jimmy Kerridge.
Henry	Never heard of him. Get me his number.
John	And the studio in Kiev.
Henry	Kiev? Did people come from Kiev?
John	Oh. No. Just one. Not important.
Henry	When did he come?
John	A while – I don't know.

Pause

Henry   Laura?

Pause

You stupid fucking idiot. I don't believe – have you any idea? – you are a total disaster. I said to Stella – I mean in God's name how can you possibly? – I just don't believe this. Do you realise what happens? My campaign is ruined, Stella's done for, the Green leadership has shit all over them. And you, mate, you – I don't know what Stella sees in you, all this poet/priest/charisma crap – you are going to end up in jail, if I don't kill you before you get there. But no-one will care, because you are just a poncey pillock of poetry shit on the heel of some tart's Louboutin. Christ almighty. Give me that number and come with me.

Act Five

Scene One

South Thanet, Council Chamber, Margate. On stage are Laura, Stella, Formio and Amelia, an outside broadcast floor manager.

Amelia Three minutes, ladies and gentlemen, please.

Exit Amelia

Laura Professor, Mr Formio, you know the format. It's a simple debate, opening statement, response, cross-question, then open to the floor, followed by final statements. Then a vote from people in the hall and the audience at home – completely unscientific of course.

Formio But telling, Laura. We've done pretty well in some of the other constituencies. Have you watched them, Professor?

Stella I have, Mr Formio.

Enter Amelia

Amelia Can we make our way onto the stage, please, ladies and gentlemen? Laura, we'll have Stella on your right and Mr Formio on the left. Can we have lights up, please? Laura, quick sound check please.

Formio Laura can be tough, you know, Stella – if I may. We probably have more to fear from her than from each other.

Laura Testing, testing, one, two, three, four. Testing, testing.

Amelia Is that OK? OK? Fine.

Stella I am committed, Mr Formio. I have no fear.

Formio   Well, good luck to you, Stella.

Stella   Thank you. And to you.

Amelia   Clear the set please. Ready Laura?

Laura   Ready, Professor? Mr Formio?

Formio   Away you go, Laura.

Laura   Yes, Amelia.

Amelia   Three, two, one. And.

Scene Two

South Thanet, Council Chamber, Margate. On stage are Laura, Stella and Formio.

Laura   Ladies and gentlemen, welcome to the BBC's Constituency Hustings. The rules are simple – one candidate makes an opening statement, the opponent responds and then I moderate the following discussion to ensure that we don't come to blows. After the final exchanges we take a straw poll from you the audience, here in the hall and from our audience at home by phone or on Twitter, to tell us, unscientifically of course, who has won the argument. I am going to ask Professor Herbert to begin. Your opening statement please.

Stella   Thank you Laura. Ladies and gentlemen, I believe we are steadily reducing the lead with which Mr Formio began this campaign and we shall be first past the post on election night.
                  The Greens' programme is very clear – a sustainable economy, social justice and active membership of a reformed European Union. More jobs in green industries, a serious battle against

Act Five Scene Two 73

climate change and inequality. And we believe deeply in Britain's active place within the great family of peaceful European nations.

Mr Formio's position is unhelpful. His misleading focus on immigration has damaged our public discourse. Everyone, born here or a visitor to our country, is an intelligent human being with feelings, with whom one can work out a way of living together – and this is one of the great glories of human society. The petty, spiteful divisiveness stirred up by Mr Formio's supporters brings shame upon Britain here at home and in the eyes of the world.

Twenty-first-century Europe is an extraordinary achievement of peace. The last and bloodiest fight was a European civil war, the Second World War, in which the people of South Thanet played a heroic role in the front line of the Battle of Britain. But in the seventy years since, we have had peace in Europe. Although we disagree, argue, have different interests, we always compromise. Nothing would be more detrimental to the fortunes of Britain, and to the voters of this constituency, than a frightened, thoughtless rush to leave Europe.

Laura Thank you Professor Herbert. Mr Formio, your opening statement, please.

Formio Thank you, Laura, and good evening ladies and gentlemen. Well, that was very interesting from an incomer to South Thanet. Listening to Professor Herbert lecturing us as though we were just out of school suggests that she hasn't learnt much from her father about what being a local constituency MP really means.

Laura Mr Formio, your statement please.

Formio My statement is very clear and the people of South Thanet know exactly what it is, since the polls show us to be in a commanding lead. 'Take the nonsense out of politics', people say. Get us out of Europe and let us deal with our problems and our great opportunities in our own British way, the way we are familiar with, the way our mothers and fathers, who fought in the professor's so-called civil war, got on with. She said nothing about the issues that matter to the people – jobs, housing, good schools, fair taxes. Which young family is looking forward to moving into their first home at a reasonable price they can afford? And when they are looking for jobs, why should they have to compete with 400 million other people who come from faraway places that happen to be members of the EU and can come here at will and and undercut local people? We don't need high taxes for mad schemes like HS2, we don't need high taxes to pay for useless foreign aid to places no-one has ever heard of, we don't need high taxes to pay billions into European coffers, we don't need Westminster telling us what to do, and above all we don't need Europe telling us what to do.

Laura   Thank you, Mr Formio. Professor Herbert, your questions to Mr Formio.

Stella   Where to begin? Mr Formio's statement contains so many knee-jerks that he reminds me of a flailing puppet. You make completely unjustified statements about the cost of immigrants coming to this country that feed the worst prejudices of an anxious group of people in our society.

Laura   Is this a question, Professor?

Stella   This is the only policy that people recognize from your party. The BIP is a one-policy party with no plan across the range of issues that voters have a right to expect.

Formio   Thank you for another lesson, Professor. I must say this is typical of your set's approach to politics.

Act Five Scene Two   75

Stella   My set?

Laura   Mr Formio, please address the professor's points.

Formio   We are governed by a tiny coterie of inbred Etonians who all studied PPE at Oxford – your subject, I believe, Professor – who all marry each other and are totally out of touch with the way ordinary people live their lives. We are not against immigration at all. We welcome skilled people from all over the world who can add value to our economy, learn the language and pay their taxes.

Stella   And most of them do, as you well know.

Formio   What we are against, and will fight to our dying breath to change, is the damage to the standard of living of people on basic incomes – the majority of our society, Professor – that is caused by waves of people coming from eastern Europe. But we are tied to the stake in Europe, and nothing will change until we get ourselves out of that damned political prison.

Stella   The hypocrisy is breathtaking. You rail against Europe, yet you and your fellow MEPs suck taxpayers' money out of the European budget on an astonishing scale.

Formio   We claim our legitimate expenses.

Stella   You speak piously of low-paid workers, but you draw a salary from Europe of 96,000 euros, you claim for first-class travel, you have an allowance for every day you are on official business, pension and medical insurance. You get an astonishing 300,000 euros a year for an office and staff.

Pause

Formio   Stella, you're new to politics.

Stella My father –

Formio You have a small team around you.

Stella I am very grateful for how hard they work.

Formio One of them is a poet.

Stella John Dove is well-known as a writer and a thinker.

Formio He lectures your students.

Stella He is very popular among the younger generation. Unlike your own party, which appeals –

Formio He is studying for the priesthood, I believe.

Laura Mr Formio, please come to the point, we are running out of time.

Formio The point, Laura, is that this poet, this priest, this shining light to the youth of today, is a pornographer.

Laura Mr Formio, we are in public, and on air.

Formio You should know, ladies and gentlemen, that Professor Herbert's spokesman, when he is not making elegant speeches about liberty, is actively engaged in making tripleX films for distribution in hotel rooms around the world.

Stella That's a lie.

Formio I defend his right to do what he likes, Stella, but the public should know what sort of people are in your team.

Stella I know nothing about these obscene and ridiculous allegations. But I do know that you bring our entire public discourse into disrepute. That you take the

	low road, the popular chatter in the gutter, you paint your vanity in British colours –
Formio	And you know another thing, Stella.
Stella	I know that you have no –
Laura	That's enough, Mr Formio. I have to close the discussion, you have overstepped the mark –
Formio	And you, Laura, I gather you might be running into trouble with the authorities over a package of false passports that you carried to Kiev.
Laura	That's completely untrue –
Formio	And that John Dove gave you the package.
Laura	Cut the broadcast feed, please. Cut it now. Now.
Formio	Ladies and gentlemen, you might also wish to know that Laura and Stella are close friends. That Stella's mother, Lady Mary Herbert, is highly connected within the British social and political establishment, that this coterie –

Exeunt Stella and Laura

– now fleeing the field of battle, is the reason that Britain is in such a mess. That is the reason why my colleagues and I have appreciated your support at the elections and why we will continue to listen to what you have to say. Our policies are what you want because you tell us what you want. Tell them the truth and they switch off the broadcast feeds. But they can't switch off the people.

Enter Stella

All those who think that Professor Stella Herbert won the political debate – not the personal stuff, that's just knockabout – all those who think that Stella won, press your buttons or raise your hands. OK. And all those who think that I won. I see. Well, thank you for your support.

Scene Three

London, Shoreditch, On stage are Tatiana, Ally and Jimmy.

Tatiana You come to Kiev.

Ally It's like a war zone.

Tatiana It's not so bad. In Kiev, there is no war. We have many friends, good food. I make it nice for you.

Enter John

John Aaaaah! You bastards. I hate you. I hate you. You have murdered a beautiful family.

Jimmy John, my son, – calm down, take it easy.

John You have killed them, ruined them. All that they have worked for, lived, taught, everything they have done for the world –

Jimmy John, come and sit down, we're having a nice little drink.

John There are people outside my flat because of you. Laura is under investigation because of you. Henry Anscombe is compromised because of you. Lady Mary's reputation is ruined because of you. Stella, Stella, Stella's career is over because of you. And I cannot show my face through filthy shame because of you, and you, and you.

Tatiana Not me, I think.

Act Five Scene Three

Jimmy Now, then, lad. You're all wound up.

Ally You're a stuck-up git. You're fucking disgusting, you know that? You stick your snivelling snout into posh pussies, sucking up the juice, thinking it makes you one of them.

John Shut up shut up.

Ally You're twisted, you can't get enough of it, you're just a used condom.

John Shut up shut up shut up.

Jimmy Take it easy.

Ally You're shit. You suck and suck. You're a fucking sucking leech.

John Shut up shut up shut up Aaaaaaaah!

John draws a knife from a pocket, stabs at Ally and misses, drops the knife. Jimmy and Ally struggle with him. As they do so, Tatiana picks up the knife and quietly slices John across the lower back. John screams, then falls silent.

Pause

Jimmy Christ, what did you do?

Tatiana I cut him.

Jimmy Cut him?

Tatiana I do not want him kill Ally.

Jimmy No. Well you managed that, all right, love. Do you want to put that away?

Tatiana I clean it.

Jimmy   Not here, darling. I would begin to make a move, if I was you, know what I mean?

Ally   You idiot. Oh my god. Is he dead?

Jimmy   I'll let you know. Ally, why don't you take up Tatiana's offer of a little holiday? They say Kiev's very nice at this time of year. Now move. Both of you. Go on, move.

Ally   Where?

Tatiana   I take you. My friend get ticket quick. You have passport.

Ally   Yes.

Tatiana   I have passport.

Ally   What about him?

Jimmy   Just move. I'll deal with him. Chap round the corner. Move. Move.

Scene Four

London, Notting Hill. Enter Beatrice pushing John in a wheelchair.

John   I can't face Stella. Take me away. Beatrice, please take me away, I shouldn't have come. I shouldn't be here.

Enter Stella and Lady Mary, unnoticed by Beatrice and John.

Beatrice   No, you shouldn't be here. I wish you were never here. You're a snake, a lying snake. You've fucked up our lives.

Act Five Scene Four   81

Lady Mary   I agree.

John   Oh God. Lady Mary. Stella.

Lady Mary   Yes, dear.

Beatrice   I shouldn't have said that.

Lady Mary   On the contrary. You have slithered out of hospital, John. How nice of you to visit.

John   I asked –

Lady Mary   How polite. There was a time when you took us for granted.

John   No, I –

Lady Mary   Oh yes you did. You should never do that. Gold-diggers are not welcome. Double-dealing, gold-digging snakes we despise.

John   Yes.

Lady Mary   Oh don't be such a wimp. You shone and dazzled. You joined Stella's march. And then you betrayed us. You fouled our nest. We don't forgive that. There is no need to call again.

Alternative lines (A) and (B), depending upon the outcome of Act Five Scene Two.

(A) **Stella**   Formio won the seat with a larger majority than he expected.

(B) **Stella**   Formio won the seat with a smaller majority than he expected.

John   Stella –

Lady Mary   You humiliated my daughter.

John   I don't know why –

Stella   There is no why. You didn't trust me.

John   I abused you.

Stella   But you inspired me.

Lady Mary   And then betrayed you.

Beatrice   You wrecked my life.

Stella   You roused me.

John   Just forget me.

Beatrice   We have to sneak away.

Lady Mary   We have no further use for you.

Stella   You understood me.

John   I'll travel.

Lady Mary   I'll have someone call the driver.

Exit Lady Mary

Beatrice   You'll be totally forgotten.

Exit Beatrice

Stella   We have to go on.

John   I won't trouble you.

Stella   You'll get better.

John   I'm no use.

Stella   We need everyone. Formio has enough MPs to deny

	supply. We can't give up. You took my father's ideas –
John	Your passion –
Stella	– and fired the imaginations of our students, the halls you filled. We have to do it again, all over again.
John	We, Stella? After the horrors I have done to you?
Pause	
Stella	We both know more.
John	Who will believe us?
Stella	We will. And we will convince others. We fouled up, because you didn't trust me. So we start again. This time, trust me. We cannot stay silent while Formio, Le Pen, Wilders and the rest of them, all over Europe, desecrate the human spirit, goad their followers down the old road to disaster.
John	I'm stuck in this chair. Forever.
Stella	You can write, can't you? You can speak.
John	You must discard me. I'm no use to you.
Stella	This isn't about you any more. Wake up. It's us. We lost the seat, but we have work to do. There is no time to lose.
John	I don't believe it.
Stella	Oh come on, will you? It's not over. People are gathering.
John	And you will take me with you?

Stella I will be pushing you in front of me, you idiot. Where I can see you. Now concentrate and brace up. We have to show the world, again, what Europe means. We have a referendum to fight.

END

www.ingramcontent.com/pod-product-compliance
Lightning Source LLC
LaVergne TN
LVHW052258070426
835507LV00036B/3355